BIOLOGY

BASICS FOR KIDS

From atom to organism to ecosystem, this book takes young readers on an unforgettable journey through the world of biology! "Biology Basics for Kids: Meet Atom" is designed to meet the Washington State Science Learning Standards (WSSLS), making it a perfect fit for classrooms and homeschoolers alike. Children will learn how all living things, big and small, are interconnected, while enjoying charming illustrations and fun facts! Suitable for ages 5-8.

THERE ARE A LOT OF ME.

ANYTHING YOU CAN SEE IS MADE UP OF ME.

WHEN TWO OR MORE OF ME, ATOM, JOIN TOGETHER IT MAKES A **MOLECULE**.

HI, I AM A MOLECULE.
I AM MADE UP OF TWO OR MORE ATOMS.

WHEN TWO OR MORE MOLECULES JOIN TOGETHER, IT CREATES A CELL.

HI, I AM A CELL.

ONE THING ABOUT ME IS THAT I AM THE BASIC UNIT OF LIFE.

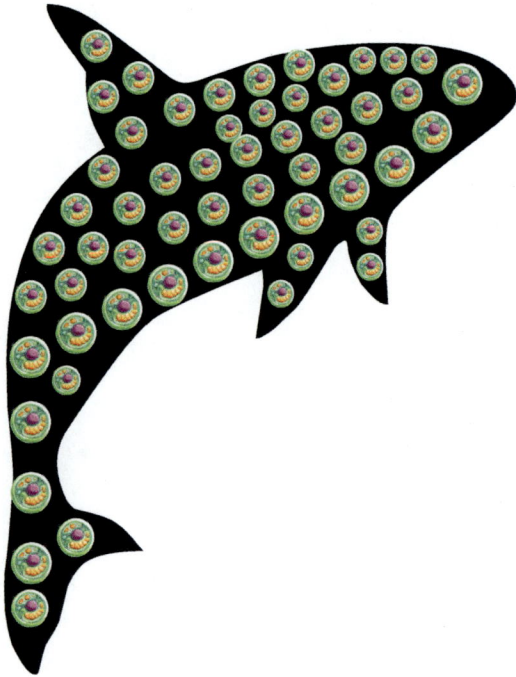

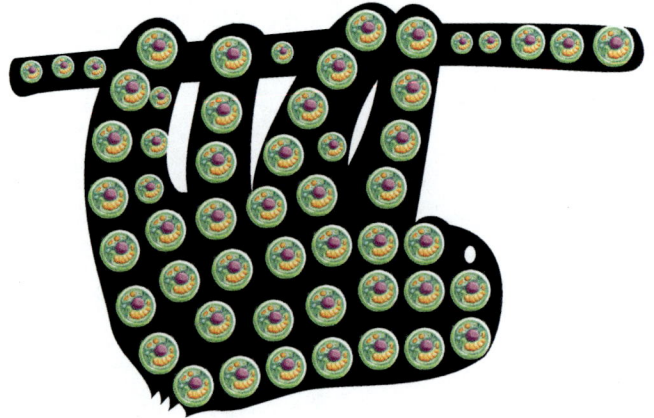

IF YOU ARE MADE OUT OF CELLS THAN YOU ARE A LIVING CREATURE.

HI, I AM TISSUE.

WHEN TWO OR MORE CELLS JOIN TOGETHER IT CREATES ME, TISSUE.

HI, I AM A ORGAN.

YOU MIGHT KNOW ME AS A BRAIN,
BUT GUESS WHAT? IN BIOLOGY,
I'M CALLED AN ORGAN!

HI, I AM ALSO AN ORGAN.

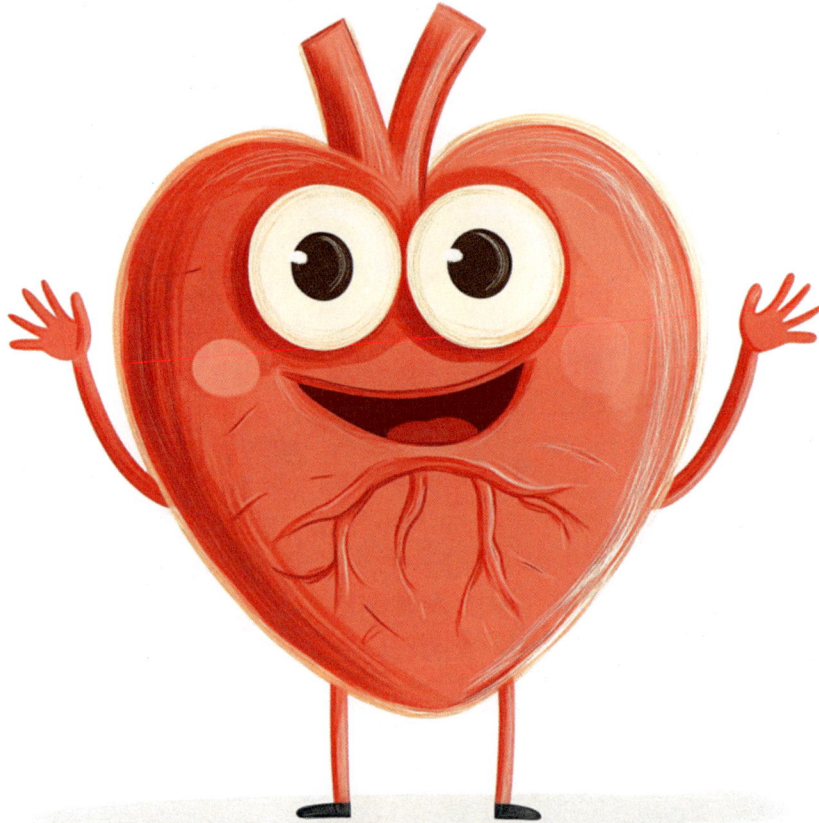

YOU MIGHT RECOGNIZE ME AS A HEART, BUT IN BIOLOGY, I TOO AM CALLED AN ORGAN!

EVEN THOUGH WE LOOK DIFFERENT, WE ARE BOTH ORGANS BECAUSE WE HAVE TWO OR MORE KINDS OF TISSUES.

WHEN TWO OR MORE ORGANS WORK TOGETHER, THEY FORM A MULTICELLULAR ORGANISM.

IF YOU ARE ALSO A KID, A GROWN-UP, OR EVEN AN ANIMAL, THEN YOU ARE A MULTICELLULAR ORGANISM TOO.

A POPULATION IS WHEN THE SAME MULTICELLULAR ORGANISMS WORK TOGETHER.

THIS CLASS FOR EXAMPLE IS A POPULATION.

BUT IF WE WENT NEXT DOOR TO THE OTHER CLASS

AND MIXED OUR POPULATION WITH THEIR POPULATION, THEN THAT WOULD BE CALLED A COMMUNITY.

WHEN THE COMMUNITY WORKS WITH THE AIR, THE WATER, AND THE DIRT, IT IS CALLED AN ECOSYSTEM.

FROM THE SMALLEST ATOM

TO THE LARGEST LIVING TREE,

WE ARE ALL
CONNECTED.

Made in the USA
Middletown, DE
13 July 2025